T°

TO SOOTHE A TEETHING GOD

Louise A. Hammonds

T°
THERA BOOKS
Turlock, California
SAY / SOMETHING

To Soothe a Teething God
Copyright © 2020 by Louise A. Hammonds

Cover photograph by Jack Delano ("Church goers in Heard County, 1941." During the church service at a Negro church in Heard County, Georgia, April 1941. Delano, Jack -- Photographer. April 1941. Source: Farm Security Administration Collection. / Georgia. / Jack Delano.)

Author photograph by Miranda Hammonds

Cover design by Mona Z. Kraculdy

All rights reserved. No part of this book can be reproduced in any form by any means without written permission. Please address inquiries to the publisher:

Thera Books
1819 Empress Lane
Turlock, CA 95382

www.thetherabooks.com

ISBN: 978-0-578-79514-0
Library of Congress Control Number: 2020949812

A Thera Books First Edition, November 2020

Printed in the United States of America

For Sammie & Fannie Hammonds.

& my eternal loves: Miranda, Yazmeen, Niyana, Jesiah (Grand|Sun) & Zariah (Grand|Water).

CONTENTS

Exhaust Hallelujah 1
Ab|sense 3
(His)|terectomy 4
Sideshow Freak 5
Era's Error 6
Male|adaptive Gene 7
Cunt & Carat 8
Mary to God 10
Yo Mama 11
Same Dad 12
Incestuous Trinity 13
Spitting Image 15
Ripe 17
Jarius's Daughters 19
From Adam to Eve 20
How Eve Seduced Adam 22
Feast & Famine 24
New Math 27
Dead Snow Angel 28
I.Q. & E.Q. 30
Apple or Evil 31
God Placed Man|Made Ad 34
Devil: Official Sponsor of God 36
Fattening Frogs for Snakes 37
Mannish Boy 38
Jemima's Bloodline 40
Torching God's Face 41
Bloody Mary 43
Natural Selection 44
Four Women 45
The Pastor Said 47
Lilith's Advice 48

Tantrum in Throat of Temple 50
From Eve to Lilith 52
#HereticHealers 54
Boss Bitch 56
Rahab's God 57
Uterus 59
God is Gracious 60
Dream of Being 61
Amulet 63
We Honor Ewe 64
Testimony 66
Seven Winds 67
From Ado to Lot 70
How to Soothe a Teething God 71
A Particular Grain of Sand 73

Acknowledgments 76
Works Referenced 77
About the Author 78

God's just a baby and Her diaper is wet.
—Saul Williams, *List of Demands* (*Reparations*)

EXHAUST HALLELUJAH

draped in daydream. I touched the him of Lilith's (knight)
    gown.
slipped on her mouth, moan & hum. i heard ghost choirs sing
from womb wrecked women.

Lilith pitied the way i, Eve was, created; She saw the apple
    seed chains
skinned in blood; my oxygen that spiraled out of cun(t)rol.
    She peeled me.
found me: *a particular grain of sand, at a beach.*

i want to roam & circle Her, like the son, be loosed from this
    land. i want to be Her
become Her belly necklace, Her hula hoop hex; wed her
    curse, wear Her Saturn rings,
& be envy of all naked planets, without the sound of bangles.

i want to taste the reverb of Her smile, pray to all deities that
    dance; like autumn wind
in its own cymbals, i want to translate stained saints out of
    temple windows; Her kiss must mean freedom.

i want to summon the Storm Goddess. i want to demand
    demons to watch. i want to color outside of lines
    with my non-dominant hand – i want to awkwardly
    welcome scribble as invitation to leave body; holiness is
    a dissenter.

Would it please You, Lilith, if we made love to gospel songs;
    reveal to the world, that jesus doesn't know the words or
    melody?

Would it please You, Lilith, if we screamed 13 disciple's
    names, b.c., & quote Psalms & Proverbs, & Gibberish: the

sin-tax of ecstasy, foretold by Your lifeline; our wicked
ways will be paid on a mound called Calvary.

Lilith, what makes You feel free:
animals, Genesis, noah? What floats Your ark?

Lilith, the Book of Revelations has horned beasts, complete
    chaos,
& apocalyptic adventure, for the freak in You!

Lilith, please show me what to do with the power of
profanity,
        that every knight, I may ride him
        give communion wine to his deserted mouth;
scream,
& liquefy god
to a "Fuck you!"

Lilith, a|dam is near.

Exhaust me with,
Your hallelujah.

AB|SENSE

    all things do not begin with blood.

lite on   1st day
son on   4th

        broke
yolk
of
urethra
        across   darkness

God   cum

              free
                      range
underneath fig leaf
his intent soils   box|Hers

uterus
in the beginning
was know word –

utter|us

(HIS)TERECTOMY

in mourning
son sways
above slab of steal;
silver-lining life
for the taking.

autopsy asks, "Y,
solve for X?"

some   things
go against nature:

      (his)terectomy
      his hysteria

  1 time of month
+ 1 moon lab coat
_____

= bad chemistry

Jane sits up
& stretches to see,
her sir|name.

SIDESHOW FREAK

Rohypnol,
Gamma hydroxybutyric,
Ketamine,
Devil's Breath.

1st man
slipped   a mickey

god commits to the con: consent – hexual?

cracked breastbone
torn   cartilage

A|damn
sideshow freak:

woman
with a man's
rib
          unbalanced
shaky walk
& garden gossip!

bearded lady.
Eve.

ERA'S ERROR

Black whole flesh
glossed the lips of gospel red
                    strutted through white void
veiled in knight
lingerie

stilettoed star's clank.

Goddess of an era's
error
come to retell gossip
that She   unto self
is a (fee)
male emptiness came
heavy
in a tattered crown – mouth
filled with broken teeth
he heard sum thing:
an ancient heirloom,
called   Her.

MALE|ADAPTIVE GENE

1.

Lilith
     mood swing|her

kick forward   buckle link
kick backward   buckle frame

know
stable| lies
stabilize|her.

2.

pissed-off pubescent
god
snatched his clay ball
stormed off   field
cried

& created her
for knight.

        male|adaptive gene?

3.

Lithium.

Lilith
a dead apple
in sun's throat.

CUNT & CARAT

Paraphrase of Genesis 2:20-22

"Adam was given power to name shit, but was a picky Fatherfucker and couldn't choose a woman that fit his expectations. God created Eve from Adam's rib, and Adam thinks, he's the reason she exists."

she
post *Night Monster*

born to
a perforated god:

a split pea
decision,
afterthought mint,
sister-subsidiary
of *Lilitu*.

she
cun(t)sidered:
softer helpmate,
lazy levee,
for a|damn.

she sloppy seconds,
leftover salvation
of damnation.

she
bloodstone soup,
& bent prong thighs.

she
infection
 set-in Eve:
 cunt & carat.

MARY TO GOD

Dear God.

    Gabriel has come, with your will. ~~Or hearsay~~. Morning found me, naked; body drenched with the gold of a busted halo. I was covered in feather flakes; glit mixed blood. There was so much blood, Father, my divine secret must have been told; red grapes, fermented in village's center – privacy through veined whispers, sprawled and returned to me, unruly vines.

    Father, Gabriel said that you have found favor in me and that I would birth your son, and he would be holy.

    Is Gabriel not your son? Your angel entered my home, as a man; sanctioned and sanctified by you. He left a day ago, and I am now, 7 months with child. Father, the only thing I remember about his visit, is that I told him I am a virgin. Then mourning came for me; surely one tear, cannot hold a multitude of days. My time with Gabriel was brief, which has left me to believe, someone does a mean impression of you Father; able to pass your will off, as their own.

    I come to tell you Father, something is not right; there's an Alpha wolf among your sheep, and I, your Omega, can feel it.

Your Faithful Servant,
Mary

YO MAMA

in a courtyard, children circle Jesus
& tease him. they call him bastard
& laugh at the legitimacy of a joke

"Hey Jesus,
can you do a trick like yo mama?"

"Jesus,
when yo mama pray,
she just Bablyon
& on & on."

"Jesus,
I bet yo mama got a lot of no good babydaddy stories!

"Jesus, my mama say
yo daddy the milkman; that CuJo(seph)
was too friendly to that nigga."

Jesus ran home crying,
tells his mother what they said.

Mary wept too.

SAME DAD

no mother: dust & rib: fraternal sins ...

Lilith: "How did your clay stay soft,
    didn't harden?"

Eve: *I wasn't born like you and Adam.*

Lilith: "Then how the fuck were you born?"

Eve: *You fucked up. Adam wanted to fuck. Father said, "Fuck it!"*

INCESTUOUS TRINITY

Genesis 1:27

"So God created man in His own image; in the image of God He created him; male and female He created them."

i.

flesh of His
bone of His
      bone|her

I could bear
my father's   son's children,
give birth to our kid cousin/siblings

ii.

image   of image's   Image
    eve   adam   God

***Trinity*:**

family of
paper cutouts
hand-in-hand

iii.

Adam couldn't bear
his father's   daughter's children,
raise our kid cousin/siblings;

Cain damn near killed him in labor
but generations   removed
men will brag about   being well-endowed

SPITTING IMAGE

I know what it mean
to question love
feel like   an aborted ghost
looking for a body
<u>any   body</u>.

I know what it feel like
to haunt a mother
because you came to her
     a late term decision,
still born.

I know what it feel like
to be numb
is a feeling;
how it feel,
to be   phantom pain
of tooth.

I know what it feel like
to have fairies come
take you in darkness
before you old enough
to chew the world.

I know what it feel like
to be pulled at the root;

when the stainless steal
flash comes,
I know what it feel like
to smile snaggletooth.

I know what it hurt like,
the punctured skull,
broken limb:
liquefied extraction.

I know what it feel like to pray
that Karma remembers
everyone's face.

what it feel like
when momma can't stand,
the spitting image
of your daddy?

RIPE

every shape is a circle, bent on being, something else.

A

i ain't
the only woman
on earth;
& surely, i ain't
the prettiest.

maybe I'm
the easiest?

maybe I ain't
a Proverbs 31
woman;

just the drunk slut
at the bar.

B

I like the bass-line Satan fucks to. I hit that bottom floor of fire, and scream, "that's my shit!" my temptation trebles thru tweeters and vibrates flames. I shake it on the hottest demon i see, and grind against him, like the slow jam that eternity is.

forgive me father, for you have sinned!

you created this woman, this creature that gives good head, but doesn't have to think.

C

ain't too many men
that refuse fruit
from the lowly hung life
line of a woman.

ain't no man care
bout her being
under ripe / overripe.

too many men
don't think   ripe,
is good enough.

JARIUS'S DAUGHTERS

Jarius

women wander roads,
wonder if Jesus
will make way
to your home

      where X marks the scarlet spot

their bodies come
drowning
fresh   as Red Sea Salt
over left shoulder

the devil,
pinched for time,
forsakes his foreplay,

& now
wish-wrecked women roam

outside of the trinity
they prey,
to brush against,
a Jinni.

FROM ADAM TO EVE

Dearest Sister,
      I will be returning soon from visiting Father. I begged his forgiveness and told him we are very sorry for having gone against the word. Father says we can never return. When I left, I saw him laughing and talking with the serpent. I think they're lonely without us, but I shall trouble him no more.

      I miss you dearly! By the time you get this letter, I shall be a day away from ...

Honey,
I'm home!

put that devilish perfume on,
a rose thorn in each heel;
you know I love it
when you wear stilettos.

you've been soaking fig all night,
slip on your oil lamp soot panties

put hand
here
below abdomen   /

break
           rib

claw for heart
stroke rod & staff

snap   torso
red

see
pharaoh's army
                      cuming
hear

"fuuuuuuuuuuKYouuuuuuuuuu!"

slide on over here
& let Zaddy hold you.

(Sin)cerely,
Your Bruh,

Adam

HOW EVE SEDUCED ADAM

I.

    Maybelline Eyeshadow
    Revlon (all day stay) Lipstick
    Candy Apple Nail Polish
    Yaki Weave
    Victoria's Secret
    Palmer's Cocoa Butter Lotion
    Name tatted on privacy

*gave head cuz the Cavaliers were losing
    & stfu   for good measure*

Maybe she funded his startup record label – *Look Back @ It*

II.

A|dam Newport Loosie:
Gubment name, De'Kjuan Jenkinz

He ain't ever did no real
time behind bars,
he just raps from bedsheets
over beats…

drop it like it's hot
bend ova   touch ur toes
back it up thot
turn roun'   get low

    kneel low
    real low
don't tella nigga no!

imma make us rich,
bite dat apple bitch

imma a make us rich
bite dat apple bitch.
fuk what god sayin'
let the devil be a snitch

imma make us rich,
bite dat apple bitch;
bite dat apple bitch
bite dat apple bitch
bite dat apple bitch
          bitch
          bitch
bite dat apple bitch

III.

    maybe it was something trite;
    gesture of lover's –
    shared food.

FEAST & FAMINE

breakfast

who am i
that the Sparrow's
Black Crown
      would lean
take breath
from winter's favorite
canvas.

what smoke song is sung
unseeingly?

cigarette break

cumulus caffeinated cloud
puffs chest out at god; dissatisfied
with its lot in life.

the ground cracks open
& icy its muddy insides.

sun stares stupidly
casually stuck in stab wound

like every other day
a stop light waiting to
punch out

gangrene drivers
move quickly to nowhere

a guy with a bumper sticker

that reads, "Jesus saves"
flips a bird
at a woman
whose bumper sticker reads,
"John 3:16" over
a white dove.

a dog licks a homeless
lady's face, as if to apologize
for not giving her
adequate refuge.

Lunchtime

a Lark
with backward claws,
picks up a dead
sun-dried worm,
& spots a temple
where one should exist,
& eats its prey.

a woman holds
her body: folds

tightly
small
as
can
be

swallowed

feathers tucked
beak against breast,

she slides down the chalkboard
of some guy's catcall

it sounds Yellow Throated,
it smells Golden; maybe
Arabian?
it tastes sweet-baked
like feast & famine.

bedtime

insomnia

NEW MATH

solve for **X**

crack open the **sixth** seal
& reveal the sooty **sith**
of a dark son;
how it shifts from delight,
to moon's time of month.

Y?
only adds up
in a man's   head.

> *1 superman penis*
> \+ *0 vagina kryptonite*
> ───────────────
> = *1 Virgin Bloody Mary*

something about crossing,
cancelling out,
& taking one,
& carrying one
& drinking
          whine.

new math.

DEAD SNOW ANGEL

Sha'Niqua,
too broke for interest to mount
case-quarter & fly

out of womb. purchase as is.
open-box shine,
discounted for small, choking parts
on Manhattan's skyline.

Sha'Niqua knew how to
break smoke
on a Newport smoke break,
& burn 64 cents, to Jesus' dollar.

> *She don't ask men for a goddamn thing,*
> *& she knows Karen ain't gonna give a Sista*
> *her overdue.*

Sha'Niqua,

you gotta do more than
wish for change!

throw self as miracle
in frozen well.

drown.
bootstraps hold.

dearly departed tongues,
of coined   barbell bible verses:

Sha'Niqua,

do thrice as much;
fail by default,
try to be more
than a protestant
slave-slave.

sometimes Black people say a word twice, back-to-back, because it signifies seeing 1 whole, out of a universe of holes, i.e., Sha'Niqua has a work ethic, within a work ethic, both coupled with the right inflection: intersectional theory – simultaneous roll of eyes & wind of neck.

---

caste aside system:

in the after   life.
sum|body   probably Chad
will ask to buy her
another round

a Fix|Her|Upper
on the hardknocks.

Sha'Niqua wants to go to heaven:

cure|rent / see
if she can afford
to become pure;
a dead snow angel.

I.Q. & E.Q.

she may handle the son,
but daughters raised for day   be
mad as hell at Eve.

APPLE OR EVIL

mālum or mălum:

I.

baby suckled,
& Mary thought,

I could say,
I had first time mama jitters,
& no one would blame me
if son   fell
from sky.

II.

angels come to her.

Ma|noah boy child
would be born;
she couldn't find peace,
he swung low in her chariot,
& she knew from the heartburn,
he'd have a lot of hair.

III.

mālum or mălum?
apple or evil?

be fruitful
but don't ask god why,

it's ungodly
to ask god
a goddamn thing

it's immaterial.

maternal instincts
lie in barren women;
can't be cun(t)ained,
pussy predates potential.

IV.

she carries jawbone;
man|dible & dabble,
& sum|body,
a could be baby-mama-Mary,
will swallow twice:
father & son

V.

he|licks|her potions;
palms of napalm psalms
written on the holes of lifelines -

thrice her wait
she holds:

cauldrons of cotton,
soaked
in seven day blood.

VI.

god can't take his I
off of us

why should we be born,
discouraged?

women c|r|own,
ours before him

we stuff privacy in halos
& stitch with sparrow songs.

VII.

dy|n|a|mite:

whoever cums across you,
to cross you,
give them six feet:
the distance between life
& where they got   You,
fucked up!

VIII.

Mary Magdalene wasn't crucified,
she died of natural causes –

she decided to.

GOD PLACED MAN|MADE AD

Job Opening

We here, @ Unsolicited Advice to Women are currently looking for candidates to fill the position of Fuckbois. We're seeking 2 Type-A demons with vertigo, to mount an angel.

Job Expectations:

become a god-ly apparatus
a pewter beak seagull

work well with other mansplainers
    work it out to|get|her

set an example for generations to cum
    as they learn to wander & wonder
    in women's wombs

no thinking involved
no need to speculate

    we have the finest speculums
    & our volunteer slaves won't feel a thing
    they're not in pain | full experiments

Required Skills:

Proficient in Leech & Serpent –

you will be placed above
vulva

charged to   crawl
      along corridor of vagina

slither
bite
slit|her

help to find creation's abnormalities

DEVIL: OFFICIAL SPONSOR OF GOD

Job 2:1-2

"On another day the angels came to present themselves before the Lord, and Satan also came with them to present himself before Him." And the Lord said to Satan, "Where have you come from?" Satan answered the Lord, "From roaming through the earth and going back and forth in it."

god's voice,
serial killer's
signature:

devil made me do it!

God,
someone does
a mean impression of you.

FATTENING FROGS FOR SNAKES

13 omens at the table.

too many cooks in the kitchen.

Mary as medium
read leaf folds:
coagulated collards in ham hock grease;
told the fortune of   soul's
spoiled food.

Thomas doubted:

Mary spoke unto him,
"The fat distilled thrice,
ain't that proof,
or do you gotta fall in shit,
to know it stinks?"

Judas betrayed:

doesn't eat pork,
only smoked turkey.

Mary said unto him,
"You are lean;
not enough.
You b|a|con; disbeliever
that fat meat is greasy!"

Satan stops by unannounced:

"You hungry? Go on in and join the others, let Mrs. Mary make you a plate. I put a little extra fatback in yours. This season sure has been good to our garden!"

MANNISH BOY

didn't make it home
before the son came on.

momma's blues playing through closed door

**"The line I shoot will never miss
When I make love to a woman,
she can't resist ..."**

momma turns her music off

She don't ever look at me,
just give me side-eye talk
about fast tail, hot-in-the-ass, girls
& loose women.

told me about ho hours & boys
& men she never said should slow down,
take a cold shower,
hold themselves
to silver spooned sex standards.

she ain't ever called those men
& boys   hard pimp pills to swallow.

she ain't ever called them my daddy.

Momma just say, "Why your pretty shirt look like that, you just
    bought it!"
I just answer, "It's just moon-damp, i ain't dipped in no Muddy
    Waters,
it's clean   & i

got my receipt. gonna bring it back tomorrow, it fit too tight
over my genes."

Momma just say, "You better pray it ain't went on sale,
cuz then they don't like to give you what you paid for it,
even if you didn't funk it up."

Momma just say, "Chile, you gonna learn about this world one
            way or another.
Start that song over & turn it up!"

"Sittin' on the outside, just me and my mate
You know I make the moon honey,
come up two hours late ...

**Wasn't that a man
I spell
MMM, AAA child,
NNN**

**That represents man
No B, O-chile, Y**

That mean mannish boy ..."

JEMIMA'S BLOODLINE

Mom would send me to the cupboard

Uncle Ben

poured Aunt Jemima
made her prey
on knees

staple of the pantry community
he bled her

moved   scooted
                        cornered her
to a slave quarter

on the wall   above him

13 men of blue-eyed persuasion
ate their last supper.

the All Seeing,
framed above sustenance:

lenticular fear of the son,
taught me to reach in the dark
for things that I need,
against my will.

TORCHING GOD'S FACE

the son wears
a wife-beater
& declares summer,
the only season.

day ends. over my balcony, I hit a blunt
& hold it.
                        I exhale a milky way
across the night.

I hear, what could be a shooting star
a thin skin prayer reaching out for me; for as many me(s) as
       will come.

I hear a woman, raising fire's voice in a theatre,
a million female sparrows trying to attract
emergency
a throat stuck in auto-tune, a gurgle & gargle over darkness.

I dial 911:

    I tell the operator why I've called.
    I tell the operator where I live,
    I tell the operator there are too many trees.

Again, I hear her breathy prayer through my Sunday
      sightseeing. I hear
guardian angels and demons in rush-hour traffic. I hear her
in-your-face   whispered galaxy of grievance;
      a prayer that could summon an asteroid to earth.

The operator asks, *"How close is the sound?"*

"I hear a dragon, fucking torching God's face!"

She asks again, *"How close is the sound?"*

BLOODY MARY

In the Garden of Eden

squeezed from fermented
cereal grains,
devil springs
& sours oblong neon-suns on trees

& trellises of wolf peaches
howl underneath piper nigrum,

& where the ocean-throated shore
has left crystalized tears

God sips a Bloody Mary
in the shade of   good & evil.

NATURAL SELECTION

a girl forms,
rebels,
& stays
a girl

born without mother's blessing;
God preys for fathers,
at the very least, abortions.

pastor's thunder trance:
birds like church cymbals
shake

loose women fall,
like collection plate change
out of god's gums.

girls play hide & seek,
ruby bones get unearthed;
omen of natural selection
& the moon.

FOUR WOMEN

for Nina Simone

1.

born in the beginning
blood in ballot box

father's daughter picks scab

his image, from her body,
dysmorphic disorder.

2.

Eve never quite fit
skin tight
in name brand genes
gerrymandered between Tigris
& Euphrates; She, rough side
of the mountain,
rough legislative draft.

3.

Black women suffe(r)age,

4.

Aunt Sarah
Saffronia
Sweet Thing
& Peaches

please come through,
& support these Sista's:

Vote NO
on 6th day creation
Vote NO
on Proposition R-I-B

THE PASTOR SAID
for Fannie & Sammie Hammonds

a woman has to obey her husband ...

1.

momma say

you don't follow
no fool,
head of household,
or not.

she say,
all snakes slither in god's accent,
no matter how hard you pray,
over the grass.

2.

my daddy wasn't a preying man
but every knight
       on momma's side of the bed
he fell to his knees,
put his hands together,
bowed his head,
& whispered to the same God;
whomever he imagined,
hers to be.

"Lord, of her Lord,
please keep me on the righteous path,
that my wife will see it fit,
to garden along the way."

LILITH'S ADVICE

> *her*
> *winter exhale*
> *strange*
> *everlasting*
> *vanishing art*

– **Eve**, find a heal|her & remove Adam's rib. Stop vying for dad's affection; he ain't gonna give it to you. Move on. Be free. Get & live, yo' best life!

– **Delilah**, in the future a woman cutting her own hair will be bad luck. God gave Samson his strength back; we just got ourselves.

– **Drusilla**, tell Paul to take several seats & stfu! Sing to him, the gospel song, "Can't Nobody Do Me Like Felix," Jesus gone now.

– **Beloved nameless** (Potiphar's wife), Joseph will reject you, interprets dreams and throw great shade; he'll marry your daughter. Don't be judging him cuz his eyebrows are on fleek, maybe his chariot don't wanna stop by and let you ride. Move on, Sis; move on.

– **Mary**, wife, disciple, holder of wisdom and absolute love of Jesus. You'll show up to his tomb; first lady, witness to his braggadocious comeback. His story: he'll rise for you. Magdala, Magdala, Magdala!

– **Jezebel**, women will be called your name in a court of law; many Solomons will say, "I didn't rape her!" The world will feel like a jury of men who've come for your head. Put your makeup on, pin up your hair, and sit by the window.

Aerophobia and Cynophobia ain't part of your lineage; the wind of Baal, Rider of Clouds – will wisp you away, before wild dogs can devour. Someone will come along and love you so much, he'll change religions.

TANTRUM IN THROAT OF TEMPLE

1.

walk easy,
like a smooth clean slit
break
skin wind to the white meat

each step,
memory of a past knife,
glass-silent serrated sainthood
go forward
back to the time
where need   carved itself

start with what you can get a grip on.

2.

learn to hold voodoo,
to keep quiet
the loose body
church-choir-curse,
the coiled colic-venom
in cunt's cornered cry.

you must learn to breathe
    on a different planet

learn the constant unconscious conjure;
heir needs its own tantrum,
heir needs to thrash inside the sown shut throat
of a temple.

3.

inhale the holy day of rest.
inhale 6th day creation.

you a muthafkm wymn"
undo the word,
undo it All –

swallow the universe's sperm!

nothing need be,
born without you.

FROM EVE TO LILITH

My Lovely Lilith,

You told me, "It is important to love yourself."

Three nights ago, when the sun rose, I went to the stream, beyond the Tree of Knowledge. It was as beautiful as you described.

I wasn't alone. I went where only you and God could see me. I carved your name into the water, with mine: Lilith + Eve = 4ever.

I laid into us, and floated. East and west: my thighs reaching for the shore on either side.

Back curved, breast catching wind. Head bent, dangling off Jesus's coming; you baptizing me.

Hands tied to your will; dirty secrets roamed free.

You ran moss down my neck, over my collarbone. Between pyramid valleys, you paused at heart, paused too, over stomach. You heard my intuition. My hips begged to dance wet in your lifeline.

Your fingers, a snow covered burning forest.

Into darkness; mouth wide in search of light; you break skin, as star does sky.

I threw self into you; a universe into a grain of sand. Inside and out we go: universe, sand, universe, sand.

Blood filled: floor, pews, hymn books, walls, the

pastor's podium and bible; soaked the communion bread and blended the red wine pink. The roof threatened to leave the building. Parishioner's drowned with pages of our screams stuck to their tongues. Their eyes rolled scripture backwards and undid, *The Beginning*.

The unborn God, fell through me.

Forever Yours,

Eve

#HERETICHEALERS

where is my mother?

there is no Oak of Jerusalem
flogged/slaughtered lamb
brined & left   wide   open.

wi-fi (wifey) network
password: dog backwards.

re|mind|her: of things
before the Dark Age:

cunt
clamp clit
c lit   animal on fire
c lamp   burn barn down

kneel
prey
       break
b|red
for communion:

silver spoon speculum,
cup of the new covenant,
bloodletting whine.

#Anarcha
#Betsey
#Lucy

underneath
    god's white
    coat:

hashtag –

christ messiah
*   &   chris messina*

#cellmemory
#daughtersofzion
#metooTaranaBurke

#heretichealers

#Lilith
& #Eve

& #Mary
& #Mary
& #Mary

too many Mary's to name:
#Mary^3

leave the Trinity
no room
for a ghost.

BOSS BITCH

Miss|Interpretation of Revelations 17:3-4, 6

A woman gave no fucks! She sat on a 7-headed scarlet beast: clothes on fleek, gold pimp cup in hand, filled with Easy Jesus's Christian Brother's: evil n' shit; all the things that God said to give thanx for.

No good nghz asked to take pictures with her. They posted to Instagram, Twitter, befriended & followed her on Facebook, did it for the Vine & DM'd the length of their manhood.

God looked in the mirror,
& saw the first true representation
of Self:

a Boss Bitch.

RAHAB'S GOD

Rahab

men put god on hold,
to be held by your name

"whore," is what spies
of blown covers, called you,
outside of pleasure's door.

Rahab

the one you served,
called you

"Holy host," body of bread
for wayside guests,
caught between, The Word
& a hard hungry faith –

Rahab

you begged enemies,
bartered secrets & forged friendships
by collective shame.

Rahab

Mother knows your name.
Father knows your name.
Sisters & Brothers, know your name.

Rahab

it was you who called God

Enough,
& God answered.

a harlot is red,
because of the blood
of The Lamb.

UTTERUS

Napalms 0:0-0

"Vaginas are cauldrons, shaped like she/The Word/sorcery, ripped elixir from tongue. May him without womb, utter & cun(t)fess."
— **Queen Pangs Version** (QPV)

Birth marks questions.

In line for godliness: twisted hanger mangled throats; girls gurgle into women, when wand stays in top hat & doesn't pull out. Hammer claw kissers are born with heads of molten hare. Stained saints & sacrilegious spots of wayed roads, sprawl directionless. Out of Calvary's heavy blood milk; beatified soles cast spells & utter us, in mouths of men. Be it, body or back alley — be it, whatever a dead thing can move through.

Questions get tired of being bent,
they straighten up
& stand —

GOD IS GRACIOUS

> *for my Mother & Sister*

in high school,
I knew a girl named
Nameless;
her mother died
giving birth to her;
went to heaven early
so that god could write
Nameless on his scroll.

my momma say her period was so bad
she drank hot black pepper tea.

my momma had a c-section at 36;
my sister almost bled her to death.

my momma almost ended up like Jesus.

she almost had a body
that couldn't keep itself.

momma was saved
cuz she had a name – Joanne:
God is gracious

Grace saved God!

momma refused to
give them doctor's,
a time of death.

DREAM OF BEING
    for Eartha Kitt

say it,
allowed

    on Saturday
    momma's only day off

feels nice against
tongue

    static left with sunrise
    & we woke the television

against back
of front
teeth

    we ate watermelon now & laters
    for breakfast

we bite open
the window waxed
blind

    against a body worn carpet
    too much laughter stuck in shag
    a cavity absorbed us

crust of
peach cobbler

    two sisters
    in black heels
    down batman's throat

we find Kitt's voice
cuts through
robin's boyhood

> *daddy's up now*
> *yells into the living room*
> *"What channel is that on, Baby?"*

there's no need for us
to dream of being
evil

AMULET

redeem|Her

Blk Momma
keloid of broken   high|men:

authority experts,
scab shamans who come
uncalled for.

She is scar tissue:

intuitive crop circle,
a|lien from   a fo/reign
god.

She is:

bitch brew & cunt colic,
witch trial & tribulation

mansplainers

lean knot
on your own,

understanding/it is Her
who will/usher in
& loosen   The Word.

Say Her Name –

receive your amulet.

WE HONOR EWE

Wymn of the Circle of No Middlemen:

We have gathered for the ceremonial Bite
of the Teething ~~Gods~~.

Mother, we have come before You
to bring men who seek entrance
to the Queendom.

We sing to You, these praises of prayer,
that You may open the path to man's
heart.

> *Blood from the lifeline of a man's right hand,*
> *We honor Ewe.*

> *Blood from the lifeline of a man's right hand,*
> *We honor Ewe.*

> *Blood from the lifeline of a man's right hand,*
> *We honor Ewe.*

Blood from a man's tongue tip,
We honor Ewe.

Blood from a man's tongue tip,
we honor Ewe.

Blood from a man's tongue tip,
we honor Ewe.

We, Wymn of the Circle of No Middlemen,
have opened the rites of passage.

Ewe, step forth & repeat the Womb's Incantation:

Mother of the Winding Neck

i come as pendant & a rope of pearls,
& for You, in a locket, i offer my beating heart.

Daughter of the Rolling Eyes

i pluck my sight, to pit Your fire.
i bring amethyst tears & a lotus flower
with two white petals.

Holy Spirit of the Yaki Weave

i bring tattered swords cut by obsidian;
i string my knight along,
to make a basket, for Your moon.

Ewe, extend your right hand
for the tasting of strength
in vulnerability:
May this blood ever flow
Ewe, extend your tongue
for the tasting of wisdom
in compassion.

blood from man,
We honor You.

May the **Trinity** bless us,
now & forevermore.

TESTIMONY

Given honor,
to the First Lady of the Church

thank her   at the stake
                 for carrying a wooly-haired,
                 Kush-eyed,
                 vitiligo stricken   christ:

her|b/all. herbal:

bring|her, Eber's Papyrus
whisper|her, miracle in well

Summer's Eve & Always.

with wings.

anything can fall from the sky;
wished on star.

anything can trouble the water;
bring change.

anything can be saved;
catch in punctured palms.

Harriet Tubman soon come;
roll up on chrome green $20s
smelling like god's pheromones:

cocoa butter & pink hair lotion.

May Goddess bless,
the reading of Her Word

SEVEN WINDS
  —for Mrs. Richardson

to the Mothers of the Church who:
funded the Building Fund,
many mansions

before jesus fed fish to the masses
y'all made us full temples

to the Mothers of the Church who:
in stern stare, with one-eye open,
      mid prayer -

rounded us up
two pews away
cuz we were kids at hell's gate,
thinking it was a playground.

to the Mothers of the Church who:
satan saw you first
      he didn't move a muscle
cuz next to y'all, in the Lord's house,
even he knew not to act the fool;
to act like he had the sense God gave him

to the Mothers of the Church who: were sweet to us

taught us to quietly unwrap
stale peppermints
& juicy fruit gum.

taught us the 5 minute rule;
how to pray it up to God
cuz it came from the bottom
of your purse.

taught us to master sugar
silently;
that any red striped noise/
      silver foiled reflection
could spoil God's Word.

to the Mothers of the Church who:
cupped the heat of summer
& fanned spirits cool.

to the Mothers of the Church who:
sang gospel storms up;
made planks become choirs
out of dust & splinters,
like fire shut-up in bones
of woody throats.

to the Mothers of the Church who:
helped Mary
roll away the stone
from jesus' tomb

to the Mothers of the Church who:
voices blew
gave tenderness its anger,
until stained-glass saints shook;
to tell the broken,
the hour, of the Great's Return.

to the Mothers of the Church who:
with sweat-filled scripture
screamed & stirred & moved the roof.

to the Mothers of the Church who:
gave the preacher
a handkerchief to wave;

gave him & the congregation
a sail to catch,
the 7 winds, of an amen.

FROM ADO TO LOT

My Dearest Lot,

    If you are reading this, then I have passed over our Father's left shoulder.

I, a pinch over broiled fish,
pinch in wheat for bread;
pinch to sour Satan's tongue,
pinch into his eyes;
pinch to blind
death's travel to you.

    I cannot be burned, my Love, but I can be melted.

    Please know that I write this to thaw anything cold that I have left in your heart. As Judas, this has been asked of me. As angels appeared unto you, they too appeared unto me; as Satan is charged to tempt, he is also charged to bring God's people closer, illuminate their faith and ignite their perseverance. Satan, son of man, and demons alike; we all must present ourselves unto God.

    Please understand, my love, I turned, gazed back at Sodom and Gomorrah, not to hold the breath that came before the fire, but to season the wind, our Father's love.

    I am not in a tomb, my love, but I am a memory, you can visit often.

Forever,

Ado

HOW TO SOOTHE A TEETHING GOD

momma in kitchen;
she got them
postpartum prophecy blues

god in cut
of 1st
incisor.

she reaches for Big Mama's Cookbook.

she reaches for how to ease
generational aches.

momma finds a recipe.

How to Soothe a Teething God

   1 gram of potassium cyanide,
   A fifth of E&J (Easy Jesus) / *Christian Brothers as substitute*
      poor a little out for the sista's
   2 squirts of breast milk

mix ingredients

fill shot glass.
drink spirit   animal.

pour into punctured   rubber teething ring
give to baby.

fill shot glass.
drink spirit   animal.

smoke
a rabid cigarette.

A PARTICULAR GRAIN OF SAND
 for Miranda

A. there's always
 only been
 you:

> *a particular grain of sand,
> on a beach.*

1. a choreographed dance
 performed flawlessly
 by two left hands.

2. a day so still & quiet
 it will be mistaken
 for a picture in the future.

3. the anatomy of a tear
 so sad,
 if dropped into an ocean
 it can be retrieved.

4. a scream out of context
 to reveal the subtext,
 of its true nature:

> *to be loved,
> in places
> that are obviously private.*

5. a midair pucker,
 a kiss   so fly
 the body worships it
 on a rocky mountain top.

6. a love song
   that if played in reverse
   would bring the 2nd coming
   as a third time charm.

7. a backsliding priest
   hangs outside of mass
   because humans are
   60% water;
   prays over us
   one-by-one   makes us holy:

   so God can believe.

B. a forever
   with a yesterday layover
   knows tomorrow left

   there's a stranger   holding
   up a sign with her name.

   No Christian Jubilee.
   No Roll.
   No Change.
   No Lord to lift her.

   No need to be ready
   when Jesus comes.

> *"The Kingdom of God is not in buildings/mansions of wood and stone. (When I am gone) Split a piece of wood and I am there, lift a stone and you will find me."*

C. there
you are:

> *a particular grain of sand,*
> *on a beach.*

I'm here.

ACKNOWLEDGMENTS

Miranda J. Hammonds, I'll never have enough words to express my gratitude for your love and encouragement and support; the many manuscripts you printed for me at work and for all the post-it notes of inspiration you'd include. I love and thank you.

Alexandra "Lex" Plevritis, who spent un|Godly hours with me talking about Lilith, Eve, and Adam and who made the best partner for projects in a Sociology of Religion class! I know you're keeping the angels entertained.

Donnelle McGee, who believed I should stop writing all my poems on Facebook and ready them for a book. You believed I was a writer, even when I didn't. Thank you, Bro.

Enricus Coone, who challenges my insecurity, masked in modesty, and says, "Auntie, you're the best writer, hands down." I am forever grateful for your biases; you my Ngh and I love you.

Special thanks to Eileen Moeller and Colleen Mills. I truly appreciate the time and care each of you took to help edit and shape this book. Eileen, I bet you thought mentorship ended when I graduated high school; I'm so grateful it hasn't.

There are so many people to thank, Ra Kay, Toni Scalia, Lynnette Walker, Johnny Brown, Jayde, Saul Williams and my SW Cipher Circle, Journey Johnson, Bhanu Kapil, Adriana Tavernise, and to all the artists that I stalk on social media for inspiration.

And last, but never least, to ALL of my family (we a big crew) – even when I'm facing the impossible, y'all always let me know, my best is enough.

If I've left anyone out, please charge it to my mind and not my heart.

WORKS REFERENCED

Saul Williams. "List of Demands: Reparations." Youtube. Fader, October 25, 2009, https://www.youtube.com/watch?v=SS02GeKuWQ4.

GtrWorkShp. "Mannish Boy." Youtube. East Memphis Music Corp., ARC MUSIC CORP, November 16, 2007, https://www.youtube.com/watch?v=w5IOou6qN1o.

The Bible. Authorized King James Version. "OFFICIAL KING JAMES BIBLE ONLINE." *King James Bible Online*, U.S. Congress, Nov. 2007, www.kingjamesbibleonline.org/.

Patterson, Stephen J., and James M. Robinson. "The Gospel of Thomas's 114 Sayings of Jesus Biblical Archaeology Society, 20 Sept. 2020, www.biblicalarchaeology.org/daily/biblical topics/bible-versions-and-translations/the-gospel-of-thomas-114-sayings-of-jesus/.

ABOUT THE AUTHOR

Louise A. Hammonds has been writing, what she terms, "socio-anthropological poetry," and says it is a means to excavate the bones of social issues, and give them flesh. Hammonds' studies in Sociology, Addiction, and Psychology are amplified by her experiences as a Black, pansexual, single mother, dealing with issues of racism, gender, and social class. Hammonds integrates academia with her personal experiences of growing up in a segregated city in Upstate New York. She holds three Associate degrees: Human Services, Chemical Dependency Counseling, and Independent Studies (the Study of the Human Condition), from Mohawk Valley Community College, a Bachelor of Science degree in Sociology, (with a minor in Criminology), from State University of New York, and a Master of Fine Arts degree in, Creative Writing, from Goddard College. Hammonds resides in Oakland, CA.

ABOUT THE PRESS

Thera Books is an independent publishing house based in Turlock, California. We aim to publish writers pushing the boundaries of literature and writing about what it means to be human.

www.thetherabooks.com

www.ingramcontent.com/pod-product-compliance
Lightning Source LLC
Chambersburg PA
CBHW021958290426
44108CB00012B/1123